CAMBRIDGE LIBRARY COLLECTION

Books of enduring scholarly value

History

The books reissued in this series include accounts of historical events and movements by eye-witnesses and contemporaries, as well as landmark studies that assembled significant source materials or developed new historiographical methods. The series includes work in social, political and military history on a wide range of periods and regions, giving modern scholars ready access to influential publications of the past.

Model Dwelling-Houses

This detailed guide to the model tenement building displayed at Edinburgh's International Exhibition of Industry Science and Art in 1886 was first published in that year. A prominent figure in Scottish architecture and engineering, Sir James Gowans (1821–90) designed and built railways, roads, and stone houses during his long career, including a model village in West Lothian named Gowanbank. His intention in designing tenement buildings was to produce a standardised model that would make homes more affordable. This short book considers the tenement designs, including the situation of staircases, drainage, materials, and the mode of construction. Gowans' book also features chapters on the Prince Albert Victor Sundial, built to commemorate the opening of the exhibition by the prince, the Memorial Mason's pillars erected in Edinburgh, and the Electric Tramway. Gowans was made Lord Dean of Guild of the city of Edinburgh in 1885.

Cambridge University Press has long been a pioneer in the reissuing of out-of-print titles from its own backlist, producing digital reprints of books that are still sought after by scholars and students but could not be reprinted economically using traditional technology. The Cambridge Library Collection extends this activity to a wider range of books which are still of importance to researchers and professionals, either for the source material they contain, or as landmarks in the history of their academic discipline.

Drawing from the world-renowned collections in the Cambridge University Library, and guided by the advice of experts in each subject area, Cambridge University Press is using state-of-the-art scanning machines in its own Printing House to capture the content of each book selected for inclusion. The files are processed to give a consistently clear, crisp image, and the books finished to the high quality standard for which the Press is recognised around the world. The latest print-on-demand technology ensures that the books will remain available indefinitely, and that orders for single or multiple copies can quickly be supplied.

The Cambridge Library Collection will bring back to life books of enduring scholarly value (including out-of-copyright works originally issued by other publishers) across a wide range of disciplines in the humanities and social sciences and in science and technology.

Model
Dwelling-Houses

With a Description of the Model Tenement
Erected Within the Grounds of the
International Exhibition of Industry Science,
and Art, Edinburgh, 1886

JAMES GOWANS

CAMBRIDGE UNIVERSITY PRESS

Cambridge, New York, Melbourne, Madrid, Cape Town,
Singapore, São Paolo, Delhi, Tokyo, Mexico City

Published in the United States of America by Cambridge University Press, New York

www.cambridge.org
Information on this title: www.cambridge.org/9781108036979

© in this compilation Cambridge University Press 2011

This edition first published 1886
This digitally printed version 2011

ISBN 978-1-108-03697-9 Paperback

This book reproduces the text of the original edition. The content and language reflect
the beliefs, practices and terminology of their time, and have not been updated.

Cambridge University Press wishes to make clear that the book, unless originally published
by Cambridge, is not being republished by, in association or collaboration with, or
with the endorsement or approval of, the original publisher or its successors in title.

The original edition of this book contains a number of colour plates,
which have been reproduced in black and white. Colour versions of these
images can be found online at www.cambridge.org/9781108036979

MODEL DWELLING-HOUSES

MODEL
DWELLING-HOUSES

WITH A DESCRIPTION OF

THE MODEL TENEMENT

ERECTED WITHIN THE GROUNDS OF THE
INTERNATIONAL EXHIBITION
OF INDUSTRY SCIENCE, AND ART, EDINBURGH, 1886

BY

Sir JAMES GOWANS, Architect
Lord Dean of Guild of the City of Edinburgh

AT THE EXHIBITION PRINTING OFFICE
T. & A. CONSTABLE, Printers to Her Majesty
1886

CONTENTS.

LIST OF THE DRAWINGS.

MODEL DWELLING-HOUSES.

ALTHOUGH this tenement has been designated "Model Dwelling-Houses," the designer does not pretend to say that it is complete in every respect. The object aimed at in erecting this building is, that it should be suggestive rather than assertive. The plan adopted of placing the staircase in the centre of the tenement necessarily entailed a particular arrangement of house. Other designers, by placing the main stair at the back or front of the building, may produce a better arrangement of rooms, but what was desired in this case was to have a plan which would, first of all, give ample room in the staircase and lobbies of the dwellings, and afford a large supply of air and light, also an independent entrance to each apartment; all so valuable requisites in this class of house, of which the staircase and lobbies constitute, so to speak, the lungs of the dwelling. And so it may not be saying too much to affirm that among the many undertakings at the International Exhibition calculated to afford popu-

A

lar instruction, there is perhaps none of greater
importance, from a social point of view, than this
tenement of dwelling-houses erected at the north-east
corner of the Exhibition grounds. Philanthropists who
are interested in the housing of the working classes,
working men themselves, architects, and sanitary
engineers, will, it is hoped, find matter for reflection in
a careful examination of this exhibit.

The Origin and Progress of the Tenement System of Building.

Before entering on the details of construction and
arrangement, it may not be out of place to give a brief
sketch of the origin and progress of the tenement
system of building, which is so peculiarly one of the
characteristics of Edinburgh.   Up to the middle of the
eighteenth century Edinburgh occupied little more
space than it covered so far back as the reign of
James VI.   In these early days the lofty character of
the buildings of its principal street was the admiration,
not only of its own citizens, but of all travellers who
visited the Scottish metropolis.   The high "lands"
referred to belonged principally to the seventeenth
century; some of them may have been built in the six-
teenth, or in the early part of the reign of James VI. ;
but prior to the Hertford invasion, in 1544, the Edin-

burgh houses were like that of Symson the printer, and the house in the "Old Edinburgh" buildings of the Exhibition, near the gate, on the right-hand side of entrance, —that is to say, two stories in height with dormers; or three stories at the utmost. And it may be noticed that previous to this period, in James I.'s reign, 1424, Statutes were enacted, from which it appeared that twenty-two-feet ladders were considered long enough for use in case of fire in all Burghs then in Scotland. The lofty height of the buildings was not a mere matter of chance, or due to any particular desire on the part of our forefathers to live at a giddy height above the level of the street, but, as we will explain, the natural result of the unsettled and disturbed state of the times, when "might" was considered "right," and an urban police force unknown. Edinburgh was then a walled city, and the space within the walls necessarily limited; so, in order to find accommodation for the constantly increasing population within their sheltering circle, under the protection of the Castle, and as the houses could not stretch outwards, it was necessary for them to extend upwards. Hence one story was reared upon another, until this system, by force of circumstance, became the architectural style of the city. Houses so arranged then constituted the residences of the noble and wealthy; and the proudest of the old Scottish aristocracy thought no shame to dwell in flatted tenements. But times have changed, and now these same houses shelter the poorest and most humble class of the community. The high "lands" which reached to six, seven, or even a greater number of stories, were built after the Reformation. The different flats or stories of these houses, reached by common staircases or "turnpikes," were furnished with windows, which were glazed in the upper sashes and supplied with under-shutters, from which such light and ventilation as the occupants thought necessary were obtained. The shot window unglazed belonged to an earlier period, viz. Flodden and Gavin Douglas's time. The internal arrangements of the houses, of course, varied greatly, but many of them were substantial in their construction, and, as experience has shown, they were capable of with-standing the onslaughts of the elements for centuries, as well as the rough wear and tear of constant occupa-tion. The external architectural features of these buildings, although rude, were often marked by touches of great refinement in detail, while the interior finish of the apartments in many instances was carefully studied and very beautiful, especially the ceilings, wainscotings, and fireplaces, which are still thought worthy of reproduction by architects in designing buildings of the same style. What tales and histories would these old walls relate could they but speak, for they have looked down calmly on the lives of all orders and conditions of men—from the proud and wealthy of the highest rank and lineage, through all the succeeding grades of the social scale, down to the poorest and most wretched!

This flatted system of building, resulting, in the first instance, from the turbulent nature of the times of James and Mary, has been continued down to our own day, even although the original cause of its existence, viz. the necessity for shelter and protection, has long since passed away, and after the citizens had burst the confinement of the city walls within which they had been hampered for ages by erecting the North Bridge about 120 years ago, and building to the north what is called the New Town. But along with the disappearance of the original cause, a new reason sprang into existence for continuing the tenement or flatted system, in the increased value of building stances, both in the city itself and in its immediate neighbourhood. At the present day, when excessively high feu-duties are exacted for building sites by their fortunate possessors, enterprising contractors have found that, so far as houses for the working classes are concerned, it is only by erecting tenements on the flatted system that a rental can be obtained which will cover the feu-duty, and give a return on the cost of building. This system has not however been confined to houses for working people only, but has also been adopted for a much superior class of residence; and accordingly we find flatted tene-

ments interspersed in our best streets and squares
throughout all the newer portions of Edinburgh. The
reason for these superior flats is no doubt analogous to
that already given for the poorer kind ; and by their
adoption builders are enabled to provide houses having
ample accommodation, in the very best situations, at
moderate rents, for people of good social position,
whose means would not justify their occupancy of a
self-contained house in an equally good locality. Hence,
wherever the value of ground has attained a high rate,
we find this system of construction has been adopted, in
order to supply cheaper accommodation than could
possibly be got by any other arrangement.

Defects of Modern Tenements of Dwelling-Houses.

Sanitation is almost a new word, and as a regularly
studied and practised science, it is comparatively young.
It has, however, within recent years claimed great
attention, and the results of the study bestowed on it
are now being seen and felt in all classes of property,
including that presently under consideration. It is no
uncommon thing, on examining blocks of tenements
completed only within recent years, to say nothing of
those of older date, to find that the effort of the
architect or builder has been exerted to produce an

imposing elevation, something that will look well from the street, while the interior arrangements are a standing proof, either of downright incapacity, or total indifference to all propriety. There we see closets shoved into any corner, without light or ventilation, dark passages, bedrooms into which not even a borrowed light ever admits a second-hand gleam of sunshine. Is it to be wondered at that the occupants of such houses are uncleanly, or that dirt and disease abound? Would it not be better if, instead of blaming the poor for a state of matters for which they are scarcely responsible, we exercised our energies in providing them with every facility and every inducement to be cleanly, and, in short, gave them decent houses and comfortable homes?

Let us take the average type of tenement of workmen's houses, and we will probably find the staircase carried up in the middle of the block, just wide enough to admit of the construction of the stair, with little or no " well " in the centre. Being surrounded on all sides by rooms, it cannot be lit by side-windows, and so narrow is it that any light which struggles through the small cupola on the roof is soon checked in its downward journey, the lower portion of the staircase reminding one more of a vault than anything else. It has often been remarked that the first impression we receive on entering a house moulds, to a certain extent, our opinion of

the whole edifice. If we begin cheerfully, later defects
are looked on with more indulgence; whereas, if the
entrance is dark and uninviting, we at once take a
dismal view of the whole premises, which good points
viewed later on are powerless to redeem or alter. In such
a staircase proper ventilation is almost impossible; and
to add to the vitiated nature of its atmosphere, the conveniences of the houses are often placed contiguous to
it, so that the little square windows—seldom measuring
twelve inches each way—actually open into it. These
little square windows, which, by the way, are not pecu-
liar to this class of house, but may yet be found in the
best houses in the most fashionable quarters of the
town, are in the particular case under consideration
useless either for light or ventilation, opening as they
do on to a staircase which is the abode of gloom,
and in which the air has assumed the condition of
chronic stagnation. The soil-pipes, common to all the
premises in the tenement, run down the centre of the
block, commencing on the top flat, all the houses in
which are almost sure to receive a constant supply of
sewer gas, since the idea of carrying these pipes open
to the roof, involving an additional length of twelve or
fifteen feet on each, was either not thought of at all, or,
if thought of, dismissed on the score of expense and
trouble. When these pipes reach the ground, they are
carried under the houses on the ground floor—now

generally in fireclay sewer-pipes, although formerly an ordinary built drain sufficed—to join the public sewer in the street. This junction has sometimes been left to the imagination, the builders considering that the drain, once free of the premises, was not worthy of further consideration, and they therefore left it to take care of itself. Others, again, have found that their house drains were too low to join the sewer in the street, but feeling that the making of the junction was a duty incumbent upon them, have made their drains run uphill. Sometimes the junction is properly made, and the pipes laid with a good fall, the joints having all the appearance of being carefully cemented; but on closer examination it has been found that the cement is all on the upper half of the joint, whilst the under half is quite innocent of any cementing material. All these defects have only one result—that of polluting the soil on which the tenement is built; for the sewage, instead of being carried away, escapes into the soil, the liquid portion permeating, while the solids accumulate more or less on the surface, and putrefy, giving rise to those unwholesome emanations to which so much disease can be, if not directly, at least very reasonably, attributed. Eventually, the house itself becomes diseased, and cannot be cured.

Another evil is that of connecting the cleansing-

pipe of hot-water boilers used for domestic purposes
also to the soil-pipe, thus allowing the vitiated air of
the sewer to find a direct inlet to the water in the
boiler. Referring to cisterns, there should always be
two in each dwelling—one for culinary purposes and
another for the flushing of the closets. The former
should be so placed that it can be easily examined
and cleansed; and in neither case should they open
to the closet, nor the overflow-pipes lead directly into
the soil-pipes, as vitiated air is likely to be generated.
They are often in positions where they can never
be examined; passages so dark that they might just as
well be underground; bedrooms into which the glori-
ous light of day never penetrates; chimneys so deter-
mined to consume their own smoke, that it never gets
the length of the chimney-can, but comes back into
the rooms, to find a readier escape through a broken
window-pane. It may be thought by those who are
not conversant with the subject that all this is mere
exaggeration, but it is a fact that the defects just
mentioned are only a few out of the many which might
be referred to; and although they might not all occur
in the same example, they have all been detected over
and over again, and the existence of any one of them
would be sufficient to lead to serious consequences. Is
it reasonable to expect that such arrangements can be
conducive to the health and well-being of the occupiers?

Where there is no light there is sure to be dirt; and
where there is dirt and no fresh air there is sure to be
a close and unwholesome odour. This of itself is
sufficient to sap and undermine the general health and
constitution of the unfortunate people who inhabit such
houses, making them naturally liable to disease.
Vigorous and exuberant health requires both light and
air to sustain it, and the full attainment of these in all
dwellings, whether for the rich or the poor, cannot be
too often or too seriously insisted upon. Of course, in
the houses of the former, little difficulty is generally
encountered, although even in palatial residences
there are sometimes dark passages and corners which,
with a little more skill in arrangement, might have
been entirely avoided. But as we come down to
houses for the working classes, this difficulty increases
apace; and the architect of to-day has no easy task
assigned to him when called upon to design and erect a
tenement of workmen's houses. He must keep in view
the commercial aspect, so as to make the undertaking
financially successful; he ought to have sanitary science
at his finger ends, so as to adopt and apply all that is
now known to be essential to the physical as well as
the moral welfare of the occupants; and lastly, he
must deal with it as an artist, so that the creation of
his pen and pencil may not constitute an enduring and
everlasting eyesore to his fellow-citizens.

The Application of Modern Sanitary Improvements to Workmen's Dwellings.

Of recent years the improvement in all kinds of sanitary appliances has been very marked, and has attracted much attention; it is not surprising, therefore, that many proprietors of flatted tenements, with certainly praiseworthy intentions, have adopted such improved arrangements in the houses belonging to them. Very frequently, however, from the fact that no provision had been made for them in the original house accommodation, these improved appliances are placed in totally unsuitable positions; and hence the benefit which we might naturally expect to derive is not only counteracted, but fresh sources of danger and annoyance ensue. Things good in themselves and harmless may become by misapplication bad and dangerous; therefore however effective may be this or that sanitary appliance, unless it is used in accordance with sound principles based on scientific knowledge and practical experience, its adoption may do more harm than good, and entail fatal results.

This problem of the proper application of sanitary science to the flatted tenement is the one which the Model Dwellings are specially designed to illustrate; and it is thought that no more fitting opportunity could possibly present itself for bringing this question prominently before the public than on the occasion of the holding of a great International Exhibition in Edinburgh. It is hoped that, of the thousands who will visit the Exhibition, large numbers will carefully examine this building, and will carry away with them a vivid recollection of the points to be aimed at in constructing and arranging healthy, comfortable, and hence, in all probability, happy homes for our working classes.

The more important of these points may be classed under the following heads :—

I. THE LAYING DOWN OF A SATISFACTORY ARRANGEMENT OF ACCOMMODATION.

II. THE INTRODUCTION OF THE MOST RECENT IMPROVEMENTS IN SANITATION, WITH SPECIAL REFERENCE TO DRAINAGE AND VENTILATION.

III. THE ADOPTION OF THE MOST SUITABLE INTERNAL DECORATION AND FURNISHING, KEEPING IN VIEW ECONOMY AND GOOD TASTE.

IV. THE USE OF MATERIALS IN THE CONSTRUCTION SO AS TO PRODUCE AT MODERATE COST A SOUND BUILDING, WITH A SATISFACTORY AND PLEASING EXTERIOR.

A few remarks on the various details coming under the above heads may render more clear the motive which underlies the whole design.

The tenement is essentially built on the flatted

system, although, for the sake of illustration, it has only been carried up to the height of two stories. There can be no doubt that if all houses for working men were restricted to two stories or flats, it would be so much the better for the working men.

It is to be hoped that those who are interesting themselves in the housing of the poorer classes will endeavour to develop a scheme for suburban residences on ground of moderate value, on which it would pay to erect houses of only two floors—each house being self-contained all through, and having its plot of garden ground, however small. In the town and central positions, however, the high houses will no doubt continue to be built and to be occupied; and in this case the stairs should be made as easy as possible, so that if we cannot make the height less, we can at least make the journey up a little less trying.

But to return to the tenement under review. It has accommodation for four tenants—that is to say, it contains four distinct and separate houses. The entrance door is in the centre of the south elevation, giving access to a wide passage, terminating on the staircase, which occupies the middle or heart of the block. This staircase is square in form, with scale steps and flats, having a large open well in the centre, round which the stair rises with an easy ascent. There are no circle or wheel steps, but at each corner on the ascent there is a square flat or landing, making the stair easy to climb, and very safe for old people or children. A large cupola, occupying nearly the whole ceiling of the staircase, permits a flood of light to pervade every part of it. So much is the importance of light considered, that special care has been taken to offer no obstruction to its finding its way into all parts of the staircase and passages ; and, with this object in view, the upper landing giving access to the two upper houses is formed of an iron framework, into which small squares of thick, rough, rolled glass are inserted, which, while completely obstructing the view from below, allow the light from above to pass freely through the landing, much to the benefit of the lower portion of the staircase. Instead of the plain squares of glass, the frame might have been filled in with any of the prismatic forms of glass blocks now manufactured for such purposes ; but this would have added to the expense without increasing the light, and economy is the motto by which all such details must be ruled. From this landing a recess has been formed, in which an iron ladder is placed for the use of those requiring access to the roof or chimney-heads, the same being under lock and key. This has been done with the view of preventing the soiling of the staircase, under the prevailing system of hatches in the ceiling. The cupola over the staircase is made to admit of free ventilation, so that the staircase itself takes the form

of the veritable lungs of the tenement; and before
passing from it, we note that there are borrowed lights
all round it, enabling the light from the cupola to pass
into the passages of the respective houses. These borrowed lights allow free ventilation as well as light
between the houses, the staircase, and the cupola, so
that there can be no stagnation of vitiated atmosphere.

Each house contains a parlour, which may be used
as a bedroom, if required ; a separate bedroom, and a
kitchen, in which there is a bed recess. In addition to
these rooms, there is a scullery branching off the kitchen,
and a lavatory and w.-c. off the lobby, in the passage,
while in two of the houses baths have been fitted up. The
accommodation just detailed provides all the conveniences
requisite for this kind of house, and at the same time
one very important point has been kept in view, viz.
that, with the exception of the scullery, each apartment
enters off the lobby or passage, and thus the privacy
and full service of each is secured, while the objection-
able system of one room entering from another is entirely
avoided. It may be considered by some that too much
space has been given to lobbies; but for the reason
before stated, viz. that this space is valuable as con-
stituting the lungs, so to speak, of the house, it is
indispensable for the health of the inmates. In connection with this it will be noticed that the upper part
of a portion of the lobby is used for the cistern accom-

modation, while the lower part of the wall of the lobby can be utilised as a cloak-room.

There can be no doubt that in the arrangement and construction of any house in which human beings are expected to dwell, its sanitation is a matter of the very highest importance, and should never be lost sight of from the moment the site is selected until the building is finished and furnished. In the selection of the site, in digging the foundations, in arranging the plan, in designing the elevations, in choosing the materials for construction, at every step and every turn, sanitary science has its word to say ; and he is a wise man who listens carefully to her teachings, and considers in a rational way how he can best secure the health, comfort, and happiness of those whom his buildings are destined to shelter. Such timely consideration will not make his buildings one whit more costly, but will render them much more valuable ; and, let them once get a good name, he will never lack tenants—and what is more, tenants who are likely to appreciate the advantages offered, and be able to pay their rents.

Of late years a vast amount of attention has been devoted to sanitation by physiologists, medical men, and engineers, and Sanitary Engineering has become a special profession by itself. To practise as a sanitary engineer involves great responsibility, and it is to be

B

feared that many have appropriated that title who are quite unfit, from want of the necessary study, to give sound and reliable advice. If it is only a question of drains, one may think any practical builder or plumber can advise him and keep him right, without a fee; but this, however, is a great mistake. Let him employ a properly qualified person, be he architect, engineer, builder, or plumber, who has taken the necessary trouble by hard study to master the main principles on which the science of sanitation is founded, and a reasonable fee will not be thrown away; on the contrary, such good advice is likely in the long-run to save expense, and even further, to become a source of actual profit.

SITE AND FOUNDATIONS.

Now let us apply these remarks to the dwellings under review. Having selected the site for them, we desire to make them perfectly secure from any emanations which may arise from the soil or subsoil on which they are to be built. A house built on soil, and not protected against the emanations which may arise from organic matter contained in that soil, owing to the action of the heated atmosphere of the dwelling, may be contaminated with the gaseous products of organic decomposition. To prevent this, we lay a course of concrete, asphalte, or bitumen over the

whole site occupied by our building. In the present
case concrete has been adopted, and the result is
that the houses on the ground floor will be always
dry, fresh, and healthy. From the under side of the
joisting to the surface of the concrete there is an open
space of one foot deep, ventilated by apertures, in the
base course of the building, so as to prevent any stagnation of air.

DRAINAGE ARRANGEMENTS.

The next consideration is the arrangement of the
drains and sewers. These must be placed quite clear
of the outside walls. In detached or semi-detached
houses or blocks of houses, there can be no excuse
for any drain ever entering within the precincts of
the outer walls. No matter where the main sewer
is situated, the house drains can always be brought
round by one side or another, and kept a sufficient
distance clear of the foundations to insure the safety
of the pipe should there be any settlement or sink-
ing of the founds. Should any accident happen to
the pipe, such as the breaking of a tube, the giving
way of a joint, or the choking of the drain itself,
it can always be easily got at for repairs without
entering the house. Those who have had experience
of drainage operations in the interior of a house can
well appreciate all the misery which accompanies such

an operation—on account of the serious risk of sickness and disease, from the filth and wretched discomfort which it is sure to entail. In continuous streets it is not always possible to dispense with drains below the tenement, where soil-pipes at the back of the houses have to be connected with the public sewer in the street in front of them ; but in this case the drain should be formed of strong cast-iron pipes, jointed with lead, and well calked ; carefully laid on a foundation of concrete, so as to insure the permanency of its gradient in the right direction ; and wherever such a drain passes through walls or partitions, sufficient space should be left above it—that is, between it and the lintelling of the opening—to save the pipe from any disturbance should the walls or partitions settle down. The drains of the houses which we are now considering have been laid with very special care, of glazed fireclay tubes five inches in diameter, with all the requisite bends and offsets. The joints have been formed with cement mortar, care being taken that the cement fills the joints all round, and not, as is sometimes the case, the upper or seen portion only. Another point requiring close attention which has here not been lost sight of, is the removal of the cement ring which is squeezed into the interior of the pipe when making the joint, and which, if not carefully removed, forms an obstruction to the flow of the sewage, and may eventually be the cause of

a complete choke. The clearing away of this cement is
easily effected by using a mould filling the full bore of
the pipe, and drawing it forward as each joint is made.
This precaution should never be omitted by the workmen. At the back of the houses one of the soil-pipes
from the sinks, baths, and tubs empties over a disconnecting-trap, and is thus freely ventilated. This
disconnecting-trap is joined to a branch drain, which
meets the central soil-pipe from the closets in an
open manhole. The second of the two waste-pipes
discharges into a flush-tank, the outlet of which is
connected to the adjacent w-c. drain upon the
upper side of the open manhole. The arrangement in this manhole is worthy of attention. It
is a trap manhole, effectually securing the discon-
nection of the house drains and connected piping
from the public sewer, into which their discharge
passes. The central soil-pipe, on reaching it, is
reduced to a trough, so that, the upper portion
being removed, the sewage can be seen running.
The side-pipes just mentioned are similarly treated,
so that, on looking into the manhole, a glance will
show if these pipes are in proper working order, and
any defect becomes at once apparent. There are also
inspection-eyes built at such points where bends occur,
from which the intervening straight lengths can be
easily inspected. The manhole and these inspection-

eyes are built of brick, on a foundation of concrete, and are faced on the inside with enamelled brick, giving them a particularly clean appearance. The use of such bricks is to be greatly commended, for although in large works the expense attendant on their introduction would be considerable, yet in a small matter such as this the extra cost is scarcely appreciable, while the benefits to be derived in sweetness and cleanliness are of a very marked nature.

Special attention is called to what is a valuable accessory in connection with drains—that is, of having a self-acting flushing-tank, which at intervals sweeps the drain to its full size, not only cleansing it from all impurities, but doing what is equally import-ant—forcing out the stagnant or dangerous gases which meanwhile may have been generated. The two in use in this case are Doulton's automatic tank, which works well, and one devised by the architect, which may be designated a "Tilting Bucket Flushing-tank," made of galvanised steel plates. Very simple in its construction, and giving an immediate and rapid flush of great velocity and scour, it is also comparatively inexpensive, not likely to get out of gear, and capable of adaptation to any system of house drainage. The ventilation and flushing of drains, both main and sub-sidiary, is of such importance, that the wonder is that Burgh Engineers and others in charge of the drainage

of populous places do not more generally adopt some
simple and sure method such as is here indicated.

With such a system as that just described it becomes
almost essential that the accommodation should be so
arranged that all lavatories, tubs, sinks, and closets
should be located on the outer walls, rendering the leads
from them to the down soil-pipes on the outside as short
as possible. It is a great mistake to have to convey a
pipe from any of these conveniences across the breadth
of a room before reaching the outer wall, because it
often necessitates the cutting of the joists, and, so
weakening them, the fall on the pipe can never be very
satisfactory ; and in the event of any defect in the pipe
or the jointing thereof causing leakage, the ceilings below
suffer greatly. All such disadvantages are avoided by
placing them next the outer walls, an arrangement
which handicaps the architect very materially in plan-
ning the internal accommodation, but it is in success-
fully overcoming such difficulties that he can worthily
demonstrate his professional skill. We note, therefore, all the tubs, sinks, closets, and baths in these
houses have been arranged in this manner, so that the
connections with the vertical soil-pipes are short, and do
not interfere with the floors. These vertical pipes are
all open and self-ventilating. At the foot they are
connected with, or empty over, the disconnecting-
traps, where fresh air can enter them ; and they are

carried upwards clear of the roof. There is therefore no obstruction offered to the free passage of fresh air throughout their whole length, and as the air contained in such pipes is set in motion every time they are used, it never stagnates or becomes seriously vitiated.

It is now a generally accepted sanitary principle not to make one soil-pipe do service for baths, sinks, or lavatories, and water-closets at the same time. The latter are generally and ought always to have a distinct soil-pipe for themselves, while baths, basins, tubs, and sinks may have one in common. This latter pipe is sometimes used for conveying the rain-water from the roof, but in the best practice it is becoming usual to reserve the rain-water pipe for rain-water or roof-water only. The reasons for keeping it distinct are, that should there be any choking of the pipe, it would not flood back into the house by means of the sink or tub branches ; and again, as this pipe terminates at the eaves, if it is contaminated with waste water from sinks, the air passing through it is vitiated, and this impure air is delivered at the eaves where the roof joins the wall heads. It has been found that there constantly exists a strong inward draught at this junction of the roof with the walls, and therefore the impure air just mentioned is most likely to be drawn into the roof, and thence to the houses, or to cisterns placed in

the roof. The reason concerning flooding is perhaps
the stronger of the two, but as it would almost be
extravagant to insist on three down-pipes for houses
such as we are now discussing, we find that the sink-
pipes do service in conveying the roof-water on the
north side of the block down to the drains.   On looking
at the back or north wall, there are three pipes fixed
against it, the centre one being connected with all the
closets.   This pipe is carried about three feet above the
eaves course, and at the foot is connected with a fireclay tube drain leading to the disconnecting air-chamber
or manhole already mentioned, situated about twenty
feet from the house.   The two side-pipes are those conveying away the waste water from the sinks, tubs, and
baths, each pipe serving two houses.   One of these,
providing for the eastmost house, empties over a small
Doulton flushing-tank and trap, while the one for the
westmost houses empties into a "Tilting Bucket Flushing-tank."

In addition to the advantages already noted in having
all the conveniences of the house placed in close prox-
imity to the outer wall, there is also that of getting
the tubs and sinks close to the windows, where they
get the full benefit of daylight and plenty of fresh air.
A sink or tub is more likely to be kept clean and sweet
when it is situated so that the light of the sun shines
upon it or into it, than if it is placed in some dark cor-

ner where one can scarcely see it. With water-closets
the additional advantage is even more decided, for it
enables the closet to have a window communicating
directly with the open air. What can be more un-
healthy than a closet which has no window at all, and
which can only ventilate into the passage, or even into
one of the rooms of a house ? Very little better is that
which has only a small window opening into a dark and
gloomy common stair. The best arrangement is that
which has a large window capable of admitting floods of
light and copious supplies of fresh air. The sinks and
tubs are all of glazed earthenware, than which nothing can
be nicer or cleaner. This ware constitutes an immense
improvement on the old wooden tub, or the old lead or
iron sink. The sinks and tubs are connected in a single
two-inch trap, which insures the tub being always
trapped, although not in use, and this trap has a cleans-
ing-screw fitted to it. The wastes from the baths are
trapped independently. One bath is made of zinc,
while the other is of enamelled iron. Where care is
taken to keep it clean, the zinc bath has many advantages : it soon heats up without reducing the tempera-
ture of the water to any great extent ; it will not crack,
and has no enamel to part company with ; and, lastly, is
not extravagant in cost. If rubbed up occasionally with
soap and whiting, it will retain a bright and polished
appearance for years ; but if neglected and allowed to

encrust with dirt, few things are capable of presenting an uglier aspect.

The enamelled iron baths are now manufactured and finished in the most beautiful style, and, if carefully used, may last many years; but, being castings, there is always a certain risk of fracture, to say nothing of cracks forming in the enamel, resulting in rust, and eventual destruction. Considering the kind of house under review, it is needless to say anything about the more expensive kinds of baths, such as Rufford's, slate, marble, tile, or enamelled copper—these can only be indulged in by the rich; but, as was mentioned above, if the zinc bath is properly kept, its appearance will be such that the most fastidious could not desire to have anything better.

The closets are supplied by Doulton and Shanks. They are all flushed from small service-tanks specially supplied for them, and have therefore no connection with the main cisterns for the general house-supply. The traps at these closets are ventilated into a three-inch pipe, which is carried up above the roof, so that one closet cannot syphon the trap of a lower one. It is intended to leave the apparatus of the closet as well as the bath quite open, with a movable or hinged seat, so that the floor all round about can be kept clean and tidy. The general system of closing in with wood all round the closet apparatus is a great mistake, as the

space enclosed always becomes a receptacle for dirt,
even in first-class houses ; and if the apparatus leaks,
these together produce an odour which is often experi-
enced but seldom accounted for. But if the wooden
enclosure is dispensed with, there is nothing to prevent
the good housewife from washing the floor weekly all
round the apparatus, and having it as clean as that in
the centre of her kitchen. The overflow-pipes from
the cisterns are carried out to the open air in the case
of the houses which have no baths, while in the two
supplied with baths the overflows empty over them.
It is to be hoped that the ancient custom of connecting
these cistern overflow-pipes with the soil-pipes or with
the closet traps has received its death-blow at the hands
of sanitary science, that it will never again be perpe-
trated, and, where still found to exist, will be at once
altered and remedied, for it is difficult to imagine a
state of matters more antagonistic to our sense of
cleanliness and propriety.

Another practice which is very common, and at the
same time very improper, is that of connecting the
sludging-out pipe from pressure-boilers directly with
sewers. In the present instance, however, these
sludging-pipes discharge in the open air over a disconnecting-trap, so that no contamination of the water
in the boilers can occur.

Materials and Mode of Construction.

It is necessary to say a few words on the general construction of the building and the materials employed. An endeavour has been made to use such materials as will insure economy, and at the same time produce a substantial and enduring edifice. All the outer walls are built of stone. Between the base course and the first sill course the outer facing of the masonry is built with ordinary whinstone setts or blocks. Upwards from this sill course to the wall head the facing is built in what is generally known as "white whin," a material usually cast aside into the rubbish-heaps at the quarry as being useless. It is all dressed into four-inch courses, to match the blue whinstone courses below. The dressings, such as sills, lintels, and upstarts, are of white freestone; and in order to keep the outer walls of the house dry, a projecting eaves-course extending fifteen inches beyond the face of the walls, and going right through the thickness of the walls, has been formed all round of Forfarshire old red sandstone, machine-dressed to a uniform thickness, thus rendering it impossible for any leakage from the roof, or from choked gutters, to percolate into and saturate the masonry below. The stone for the dressed work generally is supplied from Plean and Redhall quarries.

The internal partitions and gables are of brick-work, and it should be noted that all the fireplaces are in the internal partitions, and towards the centre of the block, an arrangement which secures the maximum of heat from the various fires, which is of some consequence in a working man's house, where economy has to be studied and acted upon.

The floors in all the apartments and lobbies or passages are laid with ordinary wood flooring; a novelty, however, has been introduced in the shape of a margin round each apartment, nine inches wide, and a skifting eight inches high, formed of Stuart's Granolithic Concrete. It is contended that this arrangement of concrete will obviate the necessity for pugging behind skirtings or linings; isolate to a certain extent the various chambers in case of fire; form a barrier to the progress of vermin in the walls or partitions, and add to the rigidity of the floors themselves. The floors of the sculleries, together with the dadoes of the staircase, lobbies, bathrooms, and sculleries, are also formed of this material.

DETAILED DESCRIPTION OF DRAINAGE ARRANGEMENTS.

Plans.—The course of the drains and the arrangement of the piping are exhibited on an annexed plan and diagram section.

Drainage System.—The drainage system of this building discharges into the main sewer.

Outlet Trap.—It is protected by a combination trap embedded in the concrete bottom of a manhole. This trap is formed by the use of a syphon trap with a 4-inch inlet and 5-inch outlet of an open channel stop-end, and of a straight 2-feet length of open channelling. There are, besides, in the bottom of the manhole, three branch open channels, connected with rain- and waste-water drains. The tail drain from this trap to the sewer is 6 inches in diameter, and, like the other drains in the system, is formed of salt-glazed spigot and faucet fireclay pipes, laid to a uniform inclination, and jointed with strands of hemp and pure Portland cement.

Soil-drain.—The main soil-drain is 5 inches in diameter, is connected at its lower end with the main open channel, into which it has a drop of $1\frac{1}{2}$ inches, and receives the discharge of a 4-inch heavy iron soil-pipe, carried up outside the houses, and terminating open above the roof.

Flushing-tank.—This drain is provided with a branch piece, with which, by means of a short 4-inch drain, is connected one of Doulton & Co.'s flushing-tanks.

Clean Drains.—With two of the branch open channels above referred to are connected the outlets of two 4-inch Buchan traps. These traps are used to disconnect

from the soil system the drains which pass round the
ends of the building to receive the discharge of the
rain-water pipes.   As these drains are exactly similar,
it will suffice if one be described.   It is formed of 4-inch
pipes laid in straight sections, as shown on the plan,
and terminates in connection with one of the front rain-
pipes.   It is provided with two built manholes with
open channels, and covered with gratings ; and with
four square branch pipes, turned up to serve as inspection-eyes, and fitted with pipes closed at the surface of
the ground with dressed stones and iron plates.   It is
also provided with three angled branch pieces, which
receive the discharge through 4-inch branch drains of
three rain-water conductors.   Each of the branch drains
is fitted with two inspection shafts similar to those
above described.

"*S.P.A. Hart*" *Trap.* — The third branch open
channel in the disconnecting manhole is connected by
a 4-inch drain with the outlet of an "S.P.A. Hart"
trap, placed at the foot of a rain- and waste-pipe.

Flushing-tank.—In connection with this drain is
placed a Tilting Bucket Flushing-tank, as already
referred to.

W.-C.'s.—A w.-c. of the wash-out pattern is placed in
a well-lighted and ventilated apartment in each of the
four houses.   The one in the eastern ground-floor house,
to the right hand in entering, is of Doulton & Co.'s manu-

facture, flushed by means of the three-gallon "vacuum" cistern, made by the same firm. The house above this has one of Shanks's "Tubal" closets, deriving its flush from the plunger syphon cistern of this firm. The western ground-floor house, to the left hand in entering contains one of Shanks's "Imperial" low-pressure w.-c.'s, which is flushed through a large pipe by a cistern attached to the appliance. The w.-c. in the house above this is one of Bellfield's wash-out w.-c.'s, flushed by a Shanks's plunger syphon cistern. These w.-c.'s all discharge through leaden branches into the outside soil-pipe already mentioned, the joints between the lead and iron pipes being made outside the wall. A 2-inch leaden air-pipe is taken from the upper end of the flushing-tank drain, and carried above the roof inside the eastern houses. The trap vent-holes of the w.-c.'s in these houses are connected to this pipe by 2-inch leaden branches. A similar air-pipe, taken from the vent-hole of the lower w.-c. on the western side, is also carried above the roof, and is joined by a 2-inch branch air-pipe from the trap of the upper w.-c.

Sinks and Tubs.—Each house is fitted with a white enamelled fireclay scullery sink, the trapped leaden waste-pipe of which is connected with an outside rain-pipe. Each house has also a white enamelled fireclay washtub, connected by means of a leaden pipe with the sink waste-pipe above its trap.

C

Baths.—The two eastern houses are fitted with baths, placed in the w.-c. apartments, and discharging into the same outside pipe as the sinks and tubs of these houses. The branch waste-pipes of these fittings are ventilated by 1½-inch pipes taken from the top of the traps, and carried through the wall to the open air. The waste-pipes of the sinks and tubs in these houses are similarly ventilated. The ground-floor house contains a zinc bath of Kirkwood's make, filling from the end; the house above, one of Shanks's enamelled iron baths.

Waste-pipes.—The rain-pipes, which receive the discharge of the clean fittings above described, are disconnected from the drain by an open discharge, in the case of the eastern houses, into the flushing-tank; and in the other case, into the " S.P.A. Hart " trap.

Water Supply.—A branch from the Edinburgh Water Trust's main supplies, through a ball tap, a large lead-lined cistern placed over the passage in each house. These cisterns each supply, by one pipe the kitchen boiler, by another, the clean fittings in the house, and by a third—on which (except in the case of the eastern ground-floor house) is placed a stop-cock—the w.-c. cistern. The cisterns all overflow openly, outside. The boiler cleansing-pipes also discharge openly, over the pavement at the back.

It would occupy too much space to describe in detail all the various points of interest which might be considered and invite criticism, either from a structural or from a sanitary point of view ; but no doubt these will attract attention by those who make a careful inspection of the buildings. It is only right to state generally that the whole of the materials for building and furnishing, as well as much of the labour, have been provided gratuitously, and in fact the completed dwellings form a combined exhibit, to which a large number of local and other firms have contributed.

8 SOUTH CHARLOTTE STREET, EDINBURGH,
SANITARY PROTECTION ASSOCIATION,
9th June 1886.

James Gowans, Esq., Lord Dean of Guild.

Model Tenement, International Exhibition.

SIR,—I now send you a series of rough sketches, and an explanatory statement descriptive of the drainage system and of the water-supply arrangements adopted at the model tenement in the grounds of the International Exhibition, Edinburgh.

There are but few matters which call for further mention than that accorded them in these papers.

The main sewer, into which the tail drain from the tenement finds an outlet, is an unventilated one ; and as it was considered undesirable that such a sewer should find vent into the Exhibition grounds, no relief-opening

has been formed upon the lower side of the trap embedded in the bottom of the disconnecting-chamber.
With the possible exception of that containing the main
outlet trap, the manholes used in connection with the
drainage system of the tenement could not, because of
their cost, be well used in the drainage system of a
house built to compete in the market. It is none the
less important that, by the use of properly placed in-
spection-pipes, every drain should be placed under such
control that the interior of every joint upon it, and the
entire length of its water channel, may be examined.

Even assuming that in some cases it may be desirable
to store scullery and other sink- and bath-water in an
open tank in the vicinity of a house for flushing purposes, it is, I think, obvious that no such flush-tank is
required in a position such as that occupied by Doulton's
automatic tank at the tenement, a position which only
enables its discharge-water to flush a few feet of pipe
and the main outlet trap, which places it directly
beneath a window, and close to a floor-ventilating grat-
ing, and which causes at least two independent house-
holders to be responsible for, though in different degrees
interested in, its condition.

The manholes were used because this seemed the
simplest and most sightly method of making apparent
to the public the arrangement of the drainage system.
For the same reason a much larger number of inspection-
eyes, having shafts carried up from them to the surface,
were inserted, and over the manholes there were used
gratings of an unusually open pattern. The flush-tank
was introduced in order that an ingenious appliance,

which might in special cases be of great use, might be shown.

The water-supply system has, I believe, been so arranged as to suit the requirements of the Edinburgh and District Water Trust.

The departure from the best practice involved in the use of the bath and sink waste-pipes as rain-pipes was decided upon as a simplification, and as affecting a slight reduction in cost.—I am, your obedient servant,

ALEXANDER WELSH, *Resident Engineer.*

EXPLANATORY STATEMENT REFERRED TO.

The following drawings have been prepared for reference :—

1. Plan of the Drainage System.
2. Diagram Section of the Piping.
3. Details of the Appliances.
4. Details of Drainage and Piping.
5. Ground Plan of Building.
6. Upper Floor Plan.
7. Front Elevation.
8. End Elevation.
9. Back Elevation.
10. Cross Section.
11. Perspective (*Frontispiece*).

It is a fitting conclusion to this short descriptive paper to acknowledge with thanks the services of

W. ALLAN CARTER, C.E., who revised the plans and
descriptive narrative thereof;

> Of THOMAS P. MARWICK, Architect, who superin-
> tended the erection of the buildings;
>
> Of ALEXANDER WELSH, C.E., under whose direction
> the sanitary arrangements were carried out;
>
> Of Messrs. LORIMER & FAIRBAIRN, who measured
> and valued all the work of the tenement;

and the contributions of the gentlemen and business
firms who have gratuitously given their valuable time
or material to the work:—

1. ARMSTRONG & HOGG, 57 Lothian Road, Edinburgh.—
Gasfitting and ventilating two houses.

2. WM. BEATTIE & SONS, 29 Fountainbridge, Edinburgh.—
Carpenter and Joiner Work of the entire building.

3. BELL & DONALDSON, 81 George Street, Edinburgh.—
Locks, Keys, etc., for two houses.

4. BELLFIELD & Co., Prestonpans.—One ornamental
"Victor" Combination W.-C. Basin with Trap and Seat.

5. WILLIAM BRYDEN & SON, George Street, Edinburgh.—
Bell-hanging. The bell-hanging work executed on the electric
and pneumatic systems, the electric indicator, which shows
the room requiring attention, on the pendulum principle, doing
away with the necessity for replacing tablet. It has also a
relay action, which economises electric force.

The pneumatic bells are the manufacture of Mr. Zimdars,
London, the patentee, who guarantees the indiarubber air-
holders for ten years.

The stair door is fitted with an opening apparatus, by which
it can be opened from each house, in the manner that has been

long in use in Edinburgh and also in Paris. The door is self-closing by means of " casting" or rising hinges. The door bell-pulls in connection are cast in bronze metal.

6. WILLIAM P. BUCHAN, 21 Renfrew Street, Glasgow.—Patent Disconnecting and Ventilating Drain-traps ; also Patent Access Pipes.

7. W. R. & J. CARMICHAEL, Craigward Brickworks, Alloa.—
Window Boxes, 3 ft. 2 in. by 8 in. by 7 in.
     ,, 2 ft. 6 in. by 8 in. by 7 in.
     ,, 1 ft. 11 in. by 6 in. by 7 in.
Gowans's Patent Chimney Cans, 3 ft. high.

8. CARRON COMPANY, Falkirk.—One No. 36 Close Fire Range, 42 in. wide by 24 in. high, having a 16-in. Oven on left side ; 10-inch Fire ; 11-inch Boiler-side, on which is fitted a High-pressure ∟ Boiler, having two brass 1-inch couplings, and one wrought-iron 1-inch coupling, for attaching the outlet- and inlet-pipes. It is fitted with skirting, and without flue-pipe, and has 4-inch projecting corners to give additional breadth to the hob.

9. WILLIAM CLUNAS & Co., 18 Albert Place, Edinburgh.—One Parlour and one Bedroom Chimney-piece—Polished Slate.

10. DICKSON & WALKER, Frederick Street, Edinburgh.—Windows glazed with Sheet Glass ; and Bathrooms, Sculleries, and Fanlights with one Louvre Ventilator in each. Borrowed lights, etc., with Obscured Sheet Glass. Roof-lights with ⅛-inch Rolled Plate.

11. JOHN DOBBIE, Sheriff Brae, Leith.—Caithness Pavement round the building, and Whin Setts in face of walls.

12. JOHN DONALD & Co., 10 Bristo Place, Edinburgh.—Crockery and China Ware.

13. GEORGE C. DOUGLAS, 4 Cambridge Street, Edinburgh.—All the Lathing Work.

14. DOULTON & Co., London.—In right-hand tenement on ground floor is fixed "Doulton's Combination Closet," so formed that when seat is raised it can be used either as urinal or slop-sink. Its chief merits are extreme simplicity, cleanness, and cheapness.

Outside, in rear of building, is a 20-gallon Stoneware Flushing-tank, which collects and automatically discharges, with great flushing force, waste water, which, passing into the drains in the ordinary course, would be utterly powerless to efficiently cleanse them.

On upper floor is fixed a Glazed Ware Fireplace, pattern J.D. 27. Unlike an iron stove, it radiates, instead of absorbing the heat from the fire, while the position of the fuel insures the least possible amount of heat escaping up the chimney. The fluted fireclay hearth gives sufficiently free combustion without unnecessary waste of coal. The fireplace, as a whole, is cleanly as well as ornamental, equally attractive as a decorative feature both in winter and summer. During the latter season the movable bars on the hearth allow of the easy introduction of plants, to which the glazed ware forms a most pleasing background.

15. DUNCAN FALCONER & Co., Carmyllie Quarries, Forfarshire.—Part of Plinth on wall-head; also Stair Steps and Platts.

16. FORD & SON, Glass Works, Holyrood, Edinburgh.—Crystal and China Ware.

17. DAVID FOULIS, George Street, Edinburgh.—One "Simplex" Convertible Close or Open Range, with Oven and *galvanised steel* Pressure Boiler.

18. JAMES H. KERR, Sculptor, Haymarket, Edinburgh.—Carving Work.

19. R. LAIDLAW & SON, Simon Square, Edinburgh.—GASFITTING OF TWO HOUSES. *Piping.*—The piping being all of

wrought-iron tube, and exposed, is much more satisfactory
than the usual way of leading block tin or other soft metal
pipes concealed in plaster, as, if an escape of gas does occur, it
can be easily traced and repaired without turning up the
whole house.

Fittings.—The Brackets in the bedrooms and kitchens are of
simple design, and are such as are generally used for these
rooms. In the parlours have been fitted up "Bower's" Patent
Regenerative Gas Lamps, which, in combination with the
system of ventilation, is undoubtedly the most efficient way of
lighting a room.

VENTILATING OF TWO HOUSES.—Fresh air is admitted from
the outside through "Tobin's" Ventilating Tubes in one
house, and by "Sherringham's" Ventilators in the other, the
heated vitiated air being discharged through "Boyle's" Outlet
Ventilators into the chimney, and, in the parlours, by a tube
in connection with the "Bower" lamp.

Curtain Rods of polished brass tube, with fixings complete,
for bed recesses.

BELL-HANGING OF TWO HOUSES.—In one house is shown the
ordinary system of hanging bells, with wires, cranks, and pulls ;
and in the other, electric bells, with dial, pushes, etc., complete, are fitted up.

20. WILLIAM LANGLANDS, Myreton Quarries, Dundee.—
Stones for Plinth at wall-head.

21. KIRKCALDY LINOLEUM CO.—Linoleum for floor of parlour
of west house ground floor.

22. SHEPHERD & BEVERIDGE, Floorcloth Manufacturers,
Kirkcaldy.—Artistic Floorcloth for Passages.

23. LOW & METHVEN, Lothian Road, Edinburgh.—Globe
Patent Rim and Mortice Locks, with Mace's Patent Furniture ;
also Fasteners for casement windows, etc.

24. MACFARLANE & WALLACE, Queensferry Street, Edinburgh.—In the painting and colouring of the Model Houses,

Messrs. Macfarlane & Wallace, 27 Queensferry Street, Edinburgh,
have aimed at broad and simple treatment throughout, so that
a bright and striking effect has resulted. The exteriors of
sashes, doors, etc., are coated with a full Venetian red, highly
varnished, which contrasts well with the light sandstone, and
gives an inviting appearance to the houses before entering.
The staircase is bright and light, the upper portion being
yellow and the under portion "terra-cotta." The body of
doors, baluster, and beading, which separates the dado from
the upper walls, are treated with Egyptian blue ; the facings
of doors, borrowed lights, and lantern are in ivory tone,
which admirably sets off the richer surrounding colours. Of
the four houses, there are not two alike in manner of decoration,
although each or any might be selected for description, and
leave little unsaid regarding those omitted. In the passages
is found a bold but simple arrangement of frieze in distemper,
extending from top of doors to roof, lines of colour separating
this from the under-walls, the latter being mostly covered with
paperhangings suitable to this style. Where lines of colour are
not used as a dividing medium, borderings of paper effect the
same end. Here the woodwork is kept light, the colour par-
taking very much of the general tone of the walls, and so
imparting a negative character, which serves to enhance the
bright effect of the dwelling-rooms and bedrooms in passing
from one to the other. In the parlour or sitting-room, care has
in every case been taken to study the exposure or outlook of
the apartment, warm and inviting colours rendering pleasantly
what would otherwise be most cheerless. The rooms to the
south and west, being of sunny aspect, have this to a great
extent counteracted by massing cool shades of a deep tone.
The wall-papers are arranged to give about one-third of the
space to the dado, the upper portion or remainder of wall
being covered with patterns of less formal character. The
bedrooms are clean and bright, without any attempt to make

them other than useful and smart, and this remark applies equally to the kitchens, where, in most instances, a dado of a dark colour is introduced, contrasting pleasantly with the clean bright yellow of the upper walls and red of the woodwork. The scullery or wash-house is the same as the kitchen, and the bathrooms and w.-c.'s are treated exactly as the passages from which they enter, and of which they might almost be called a continuation. Altogether, the impression created by studying the painting work of the Model Dwellings is one of extreme smartness combined with utility, without making use of any costly medium in arriving at the effects. To produce the work at the minimum of cost commensurate with good workmanship has been the aim of the painters. The wall-papers used throughout are manufactured and supplied free of charge by Messrs. Jeffrey & Co., 64 Essex Road, Islington, London, N.

25. WALTER MACFARLANE & Co., Saracen Works, Glasgow.— Rhones, Conductors, Soil-pipes, etc.

26. MACKENZIE & Co., Gilmore Park Foundry, Edinburgh.— Iron Gratings for stair landings, Covers for cesspool and flushing-tank.

27. WILLIAM OMIT, Highriggs, Tollcross, Edinburgh.— Malleable-iron Stair Railings.

27½. JOHN TAYLOR & SON, Princes Street, Edinburgh.— House Furniture and Carpets.

28. ROYAL BLIND ASYLUM, Nicolson Street, Edinburgh.— Bedsteads and Bedding.

29. WM. SCOTT MORTON, Tynecastle, Edinburgh.—Mantel-piece in Oak, fitted with Scott Morton's Patent Blower Slow Combustion Grate.

30. SHANKS & Co., Barrhead, near Glasgow.—Shanks's Patent No. 6 5-ft. 6-in. parallel-sided Rolled Edge Bath,

japanned inside and outside, with fittings for hot, cold, and
waste, and ornamental feet, to stand without woodwork :
Shanks's Patent No. 1 Tubal Closet, in one solid piece of
strong fine fireclay, white inside, and buff glazed outside :
Shanks's Patent No. 16 Improved "Reliable" Syphon Cistern,
3 gallons' flush, to supply above Closet.   Woodwork and
other fittings extra.   Shanks's Patent No. 1 Imperial Closet
and Cistern combined.   Closet made of same material as
No. 1 Tubal, and the cistern fixed right at back of closet,
which is made with large inlet horn, is a valve cistern, having
an outlet valve correspondingly large to the inlet horn of
closet, and through which, when the valve is lifted, the con-
tents of cistern is instantly precipitated, washing out the
closet most thoroughly.   Both of above closets are constructed
to be fixed with hinged seat, and without the ordinary wood
enclosure, as in the case of the bath.   They secure in this way
a large saving in woodwork, and serve the threefold purpose
of slop-sink, urinal, and closet, besides being superior from a
sanitary point of view.

31. ALEX. B. SHAW, 29 Commercial Street, Leith.—The
Jarrow Cement Company, Limited, contributed to the erection
all the Portland Cement for foundation, pointing, drains, etc.,
and Hydraulic Lime for building the walls, partitions, etc.

32. ANDREW SLATER, Slater, Canongate.—Slates and Slating
Work.

33. J. W. & G. STRATTON, Newington, Edinburgh.—Whin
Setts from Ravelriggs Quarries in face of building.

34. STUART & Co., Thomas Street, Edinburgh. — Red
Granolithic Dado and Floor Border, passages and scullery and
chimney-pieces.

35. STOREY BROTHERS, Lothian Road, Edinburgh.—Window
Blinds for one house.

36. WM. BRYDEN & SON, George Street, Edinburgh.—Window Blinds for one house.

37. BAILIE WALCOT, Greenside Street, Edinburgh.—One Port Downie Kitchen Range, Oven, and Boiler; one Kinnaird Interior Grate for Parlour; one Kinnaird Interior Grate for Bedroom.

38. WYLAM WALKER, Gorebridge, Hexham. — Sewerage Pipes and Traps.

39. CONVENER JOHN WHITE, St. Andrew Street, Edinburgh.—All the Plumber Work, Bath-tubs, and Sinks.

40. WALKER, HUNTER & Co., Falkirk.—Artisan Kitchen Range, with Oven, Hot Closet, and Back Boiler, all self-setting and self-acting, with Ash-pan ; also Mantelpieces.

41. WALTER BRODIE, South Clerk Street, Edinburgh.—Self-acting Flushing-tank.

42. Messrs. THOMAS METHVEN & SONS, 15 Princes Street, Edinburgh, supplied the Flowers for Window-Boxes and Flower Plot in front.

43. JAMES GOWANS, 31 Castle Terrace, Edinburgh.—All the Stone (from Pleine and Redhall Quarries), used in the construction of the building, with the exception of the plinth, steps, platts, and pavement.

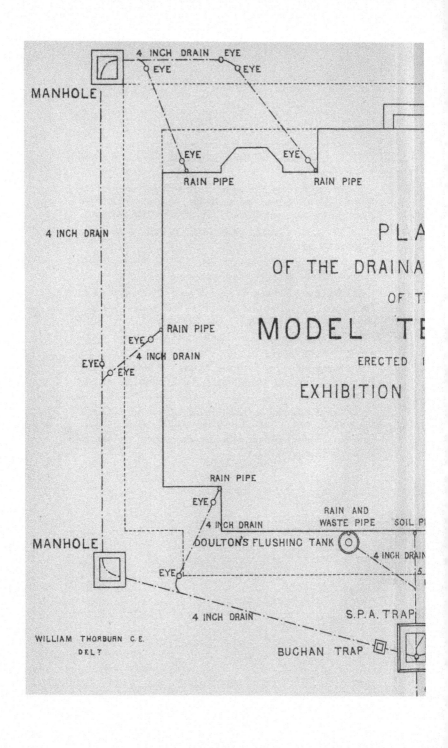

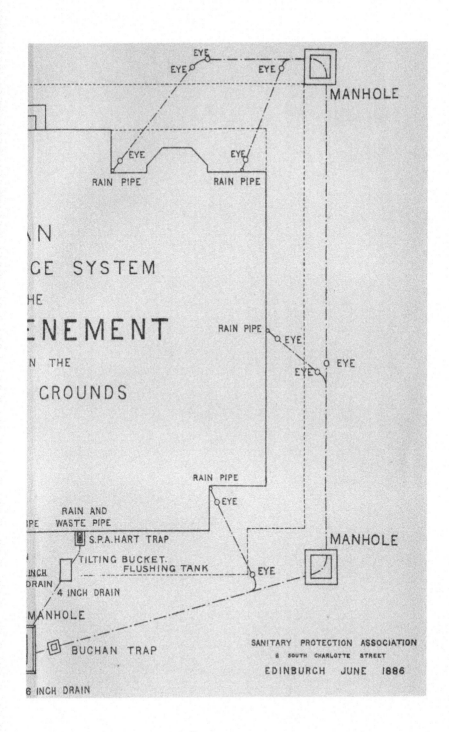

MANHOLE

EYE
EYE EYE
EYE

EYE EYE

RAIN PIPE   RAIN PIPE

AN

CE SYSTEM

HE

ENEMENT

N THE

CROUNDS

RAIN PIPE
EYE

EYE

EYE
EYE

RAIN PIPE

EYE

MANHOLE

RAIN AND
IPE   WASTE PIPE

S.P.A.HART TRAP

TILTING BUCKET.
FLUSHING TANK   EYE

INCH
DRAIN
4 INCH DRAIN

MANHOLE

BUCHAN TRAP

6 INCH DRAIN

SANITARY PROTECTION ASSOCIATION
8 SOUTH CHARLOTTE STREET
EDINBURCH   JUNE   1886

DIACRAM SECTION
OF
MODEL T

RAIN PIPE

RAIN PIPE

EYE

EYE

EYE

EYE

EYE

RAIN WATER DRAIN

MANHOLE

RAIN PIPE

EYE AND SHAFT

EYE

RAIN WATER DRAIN

EYE

RAIN PIPE

RAIN WATER DRAIN

EYE

MANHOLE

RAIN WATER DRAIN

EYE

RAIN WATER DRAIN

STEAM PIPE

RAIN PIPE

CISTERN

TUB

SINK

TRAP AIR PIPES

BATH

BOILER

STEAM PIPE

BOILER CLEANER

CISTERN

COLD SUPPLY

HOT

TUB

SINK

TRAP AIR PIPES

WASTE PIPE

BATH

BOILER

BOILER CLEANER

OPEN

DOULTON'S
FLUSH TANK

OPEN

AIR

WATER MAIN

BUCHAN TRAP

S.P.A. TRAP MANH

TAIL

DRAIN

WILLIAM THORBURN C.E.
DELT

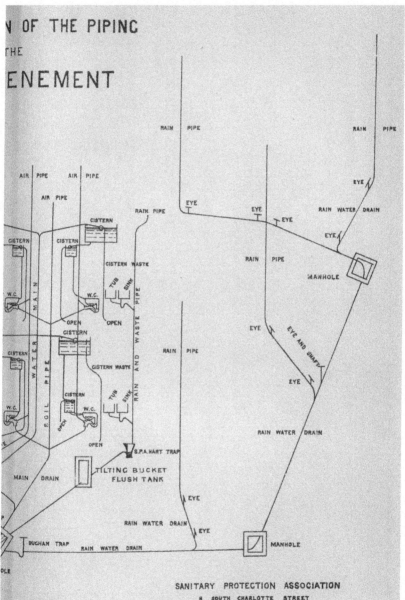

N OF THE PIPINC

THE

ENEMENT

SANITARY PROTECTION ASSOCIATION

8 SOUTH CHARLOTTE STREET

EDINBURGH   JUNE   1886

DETAILS OF THE

ADOPTED AT

MODEL TE

SANITARY PROTECTION

8 SOUTH CHARLOTTE

EDINBURGH   JUNE

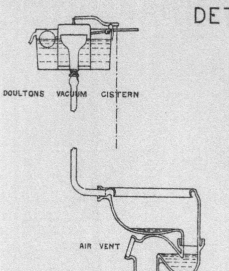

DOULTONS VACUUM CISTERN

AIR VENT

DOULTONS WASHOUT W.C.

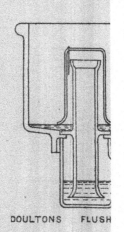

DOULTONS FLUSH

CISTERN

AIR VENT

SHANKS IMPERIAL W.C.

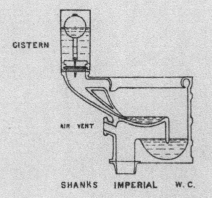

WILLIAM THORBURN C.E.
DELT

WASTE PIP

TILTING BUCKET

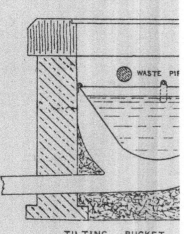

APPLIANCES

THE

ɪNEMENT

ASSOCIATION

STREET

1886

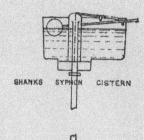
SHANKS SYPHON CISTERN

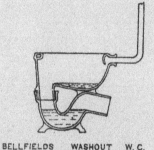
BELLFIELDS WASHOUT W.C.

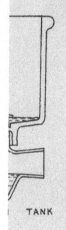
TANK

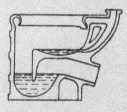
SHANKS TUBAL W.C.

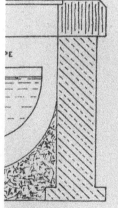
FLUSH TANK

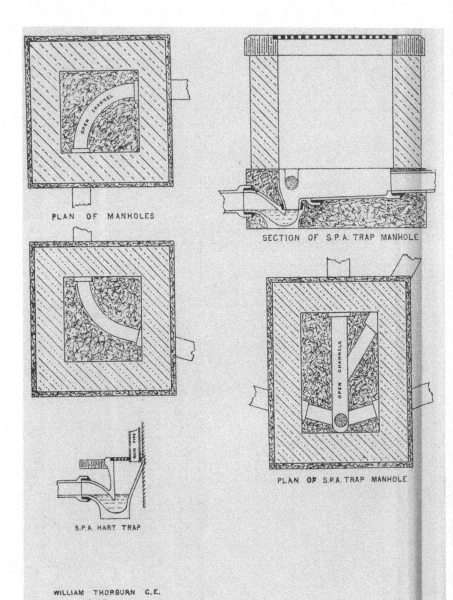

PLAN OF MANHOLES

SECTION OF S.P.A. TRAP MANHOLE

PLAN OF S.P.A. TRAP MANHOLE

S.P.A. HART TRAP

WILLIAM THORBURN C.E.
DELT

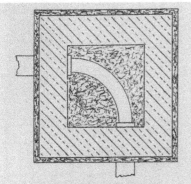

PLAN OF MANHOLES

DETAILS

OF THE

DRAINAGE SYSTEM

OF THE

MODEL TENEMENT

SANITARY PROTECTION ASSOCIATION
8 SOUTH CHARLOTTE STREET
EDINBURGH   JUNE   1886

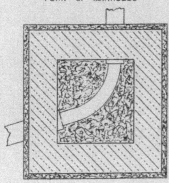

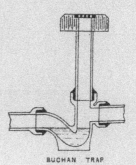

BUCHAN TRAP

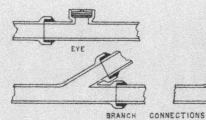

EYE

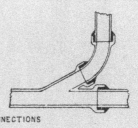

BRANCH   CONNECTIONS

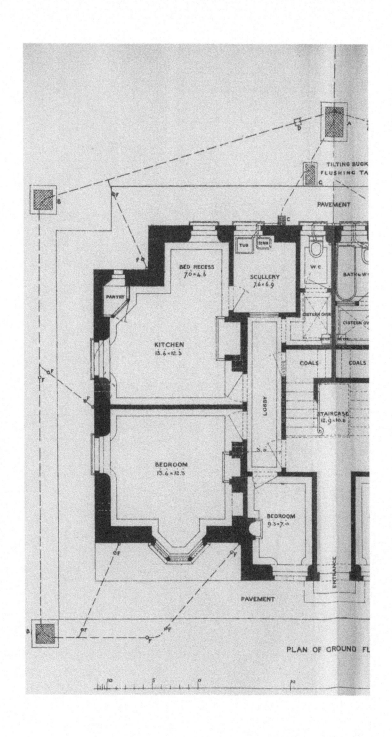

PLAN OF GROUND FL

TILTING BUCK
FLUSHING TA

PAVEMENT

TUB SINK
SCULLERY
7.6 × 6.9

W.C.

BATH & W

BED RECESS
7.0 × 4.6

PANTRY

CISTERN OVER
CISTERN OV

KITCHEN
13.6 × 12.3

COALS
COALS

LOBBY

STAIRCASE
12.9 × 10.8

BEDROOM
13.6 × 12.3

3.8

BEDROOM
9.3 × 7.0

ENTRANCE

PAVEMENT

10   5   0   10

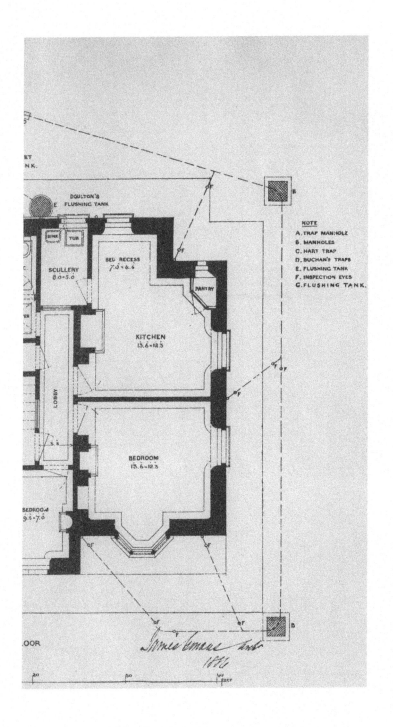

ET
NK.

DOULTON'S
FLUSHING TANK

SINK | TUB

SCULLERY
8.0×5.0

BED RECESS
7.0×4.6

PANTRY

KITCHEN
13.6×12.3

LOBBY

BEDROOM
13.6×12.3

BEDROOM
9.6×7.6

NOTE
A. TRAP MANHOLE
B. MANHOLES
C. HART TRAP
D. BUCHAN'S TRAPS
E. FLUSHING TANK
F. INSPECTION EYES
G. FLUSHING TANK.

OOR

James Evans Arct
1896

FEET

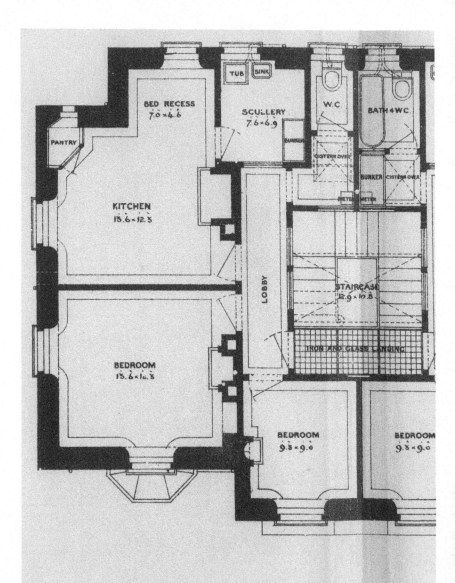

PANTRY

BED RECESS
7.0 × 4.6

TUB SINK

SCULLERY
7.6 × 6.9

BUNKER

CISTERN OVER

W.C

BATH & W.C.

BUNKER CISTERN OVER

KITCHEN
13.6 × 12.3

METER METER

STAIRCASE
12.9 × 10.3

LOBBY

BEDROOM
13.6 × 14.3

IRON AND GLASS LANDING

BEDROOM
9.3 × 9.0

BEDROOM
9.3 × 9.0

PLAN OF UPPER FLOOR

10   5   0   10   20

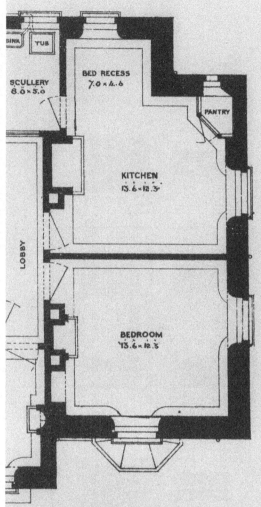

SINK   TUB

SCULLERY
8.0 × 5.0

BED RECESS
7.0 × 4.6

PANTRY

KITCHEN
13.6 × 12.3

LOBBY

BEDROOM
13.6 × 12.3

30   40
FEET.

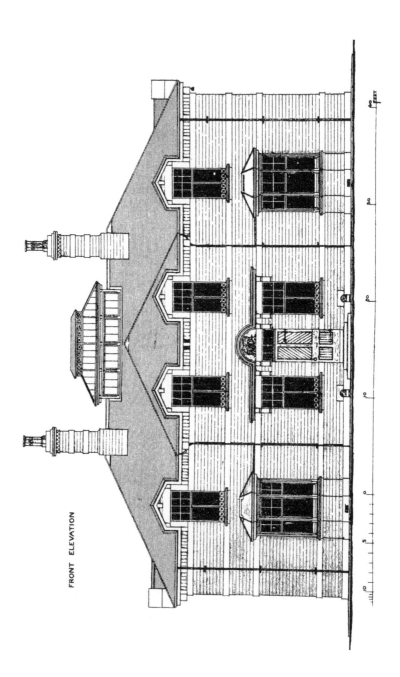

FRONT ELEVATION

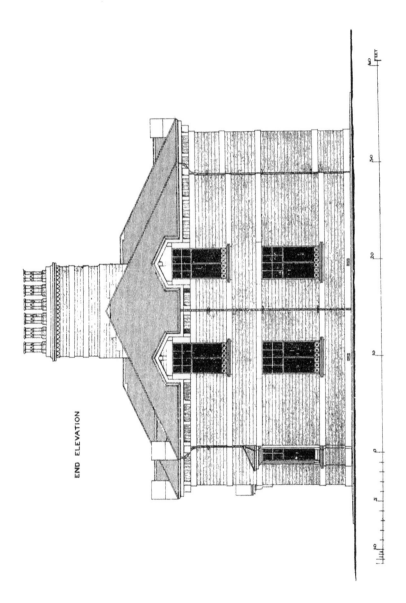

END ELEVATION

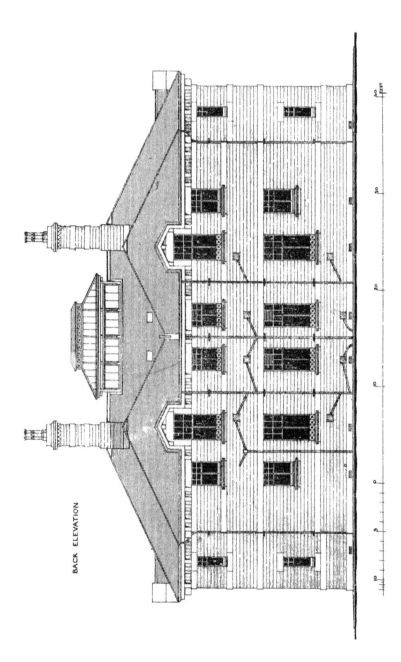

BACK ELEVATION

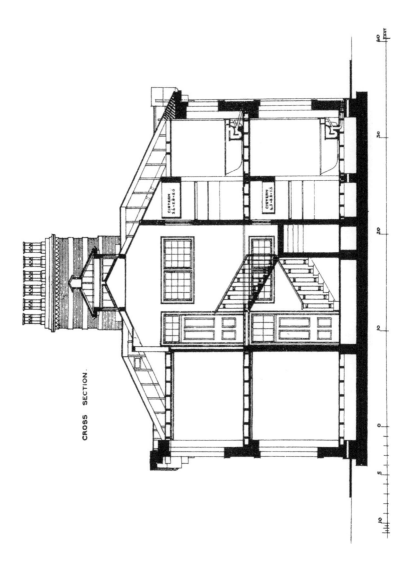

CROSS SECTION.

THE PRINCE ALBERT VICTOR
SUN-DIAL.

THE PRINCE ALBERT VICTOR SUN-DIAL.

THE PRINCE ALBERT VICTOR SUN-DIAL.

THIS Dial was erected in commemoration of the opening of the Exhibition by his Royal Highness Prince Albert Victor of Wales, on the 6th May 1886. It is built of eight different kinds of freestone, in eleven courses. The *first* course is a red stone from Moat Quarry; the *second*, also red, from Corncockle; the *third*, a yellow, from Whitsome Newton; the *fourth*, also yellow, from Cragg; the *fifth*, from Myreton, blue; the *sixth*, yellow, from Cocklaw; the *seventh*, Redhall, yellow; the *eighth*, Myreton, blue; the *ninth*, Balloch-myle, red; the *tenth*, blue, from Myreton; and the *eleventh*, or base, of armillary sphere, yellow, from Redhall. It is octagonal in shape, panelled on four sides, the other four being plain polished work. On the fifth course the dialing is cut, and on the ninth one are four shields, bearing the coronet of the Prince, the arms of the Marquis of Lothian, the cipher of the Lord Provost, with the City Arms in the centre, and on the other the Scottish Arms. In the intervening panels are the following inscriptions :—

ERECTED IN COMMEMORATION

OF THE OPENING OF

THE INTERNATIONAL EXHIBITION

BY

H.R.H. PRINCE ALBERT VICTOR OF WALES,

ON *6th May* 1886.

THE MOST HONOURABLE

MARQUIS OF LOTHIAN, K.T., *President.*

THE RIGHT HONOURABLE

THOMAS CLARK, *Lord Provost of the City.*

JAMES GOWANS, LORD DEAN OF GUILD,
Chairman of the Executive Council.

On the lower base the following lines are carved :—

" I mark but the hours of sunshine."

"Time and tide wait for no man."

" Light is the shadow of God."

"Time is the chrysalis of eternity."

" As a servant earnestly desireth the shadow."

" Time, as he passes us, has a dove's wing,
Unsoiled and swift, and of a silken sound."

" Man's days are as a shadow that passeth away."

" Well-arranged time is
The surest sign of a well-arranged mind."

On the top plinth of Myreton stone is cut—

> "Tak' tent o' time,
> Ere time be tint."

On the four surfaces of the fifth course are dials facing the cardinal points, showing Edinburgh time, which is 12' 45" after Greenwich time. The equation of time is also to be added or subtracted, according as the clock is before or after the sun. On the top of the pillar is an armillary sphere made of bronze, which also acts as a sun-dial. The centre rod with the arrow represents the polar axis of the earth, and it casts a shadow upon the equatorial zone, on which the hours are indicated. The following lines are inscribed on the ring :—

> "Let others tell of storms and showers,
> I'll only count the sunny hours."

MEMORIAL PILLARS

ERECTED BY

THE MASTER BUILDERS

AND

OPERATIVE MASONS

OF

EDINBURGH AND LEITH.

THE MEMORIAL

MASONS' PILLARS.

THE MEMORIAL MASONS' PILLARS.

THE two Memorial Masons' Pillars, near the principal entrance, have been erected by the Master Builders and Operative Masons of Edinburgh and Leith, as a permanent memento of the Exhibition, and form an entrance from Brougham Street to the Melville Drive.

The pillars are octagon on plan, having the four angular sides recessed and panelled. The base is moulded, and a centre band exhibits shields on each of the four sides, and panels with inscriptions on each of the four angles. The caps are massive blocks, having shields on each of the eight sides.

It was found necessary to excavate for a secure foundation 5 and 7 feet deep respectively, and to carry it up with cement concrete to within 2 feet of the surface. In addition to the 2 feet of stone below the surface of the ground, the pillars are 26 feet high, and are surmounted by unicorns, each 7 feet in height. The diameter of the octagon shafts is 3 feet 3 inches. There are eighteen courses of stone in the height, and each course is in a single stone, seventeen different quarries being represented. The bases, centre bands, friezes, and unicorns are of red

sandstone; the stones in the shafts and caps are of
various shades, chiefly of yellow freestone. On each
course is cut the name of the quarry for after reference as to durability and colour.

While the pillars generally are of polished work,
on each of the plain faces of the shaft illustrations are
given of various kinds of masons' work, which it is
expected may be of use. From the base upwards the
descriptions of work illustrated are—Nidged, Ham-
mer-daubed, Tooled, Fine-broatched, Splitter-striped,
Fine-punched, Chisel-striped, Plain-droved, Broatched,
Angular-droved, Stugged, Polished, Fluted, and
Scabbled.

The twenty-four shields on the caps and centre bands
display the Imperial, Scottish, English, and Irish arms;
the coats-of-arms of nineteen Scottish burghs, and the
crest of the Edinburgh masons.

The following have contributed towards the erection
of the Pillars :—

> JAMES GOWANS, Esq., Lord Dean of Guild.—The Design
> and Specification.
> THOMAS FAIRBAIRN, Esq., Surveyor.—The Schedules of
> Measurements.
> D. W. STEVENSON, A.R.S.A.—Model of Unicorns.
> WM. CAMPBELL & SON, Architectural Modellers, Torphichen
> Street, Edinburgh, executed the Model of the Pillars.
> SCULPTORS AND MODELLERS IN EDINBURGH AND GLASGOW.
> —Models of the twenty-four Shields.
> CALEDONIAN AND NORTH BRITISH RAILWAY COMPANIES.—
> Carriage of Stone at half the usual Rates.

EDINBURGH OPERATIVE MASONS.—The Cost of working and setting one of the Pillars.

EDINBURGH AND LEITH MASTER BUILDERS' ASSOCIATION.—Cost of working and setting the other Pillar.

WILLIAM NELSON, Esq., Salisbury Green, gave handsome subscriptions for the carved work; and WILLIAM M'EWAN, Esq., 25 Palmerston Place, and the Executive Council, the balance.

·The following·Quarrymasters have contributed the stones forming the Pillars :—

BAIRD & STEVENSON, Dunmore, Bannockburn.
BENSON, WILLIAM, PRUDHAM, Fourstones, Northumberland.
CARMICHAEL, SIR WILLIAM GIBSON, Hailes, Slateford.
COLVILLE, ARTHUR, Hermand, Midcalder.
DUNCAN & SON, WILLIAM, Binny, Linlithgowshire.
GENTLE, BAILIE, Leoch, Dundee.
GOWANS, JAMES, Plean, Bannockburn.
HERBERTSON & SON, Moat, Carlisle.
Do.   do.   Cocklaw, Roxburghshire.
MURRAY, J. & A., Coxhill, Annan.
PEGG, W. J., Parkhead, Woodburn.
PENNYCOOK, JOHN, Dalmeny, Linlithgowshire.
ROBINSON, HENRY, Woodburn, Northumberland.
ROSS & YOUNG, Polmaise, Bannockburn.
STEEL & TURNER, Cragg, Northumberland.
Do.   do.   Gunnerton, Northumberland.
WM. THOMSON & SON, Gatelaw Bridge, Thornhill.

The contractors were — ALEXANDER MITCHELL, Builder; JAMES H. KERR, A. & J. S. RHIND, and ALEXANDER NEILSON, Sculptors. Mr. JOHN SUTHERLAND superintended the work on behalf of the Master Builders, and Mr. JAMES HOLLAND on behalf of the Operative Masons.

E

ELECTRIC TRAMWAY.

THIS Tramway was laid down for the purpose of exhibiting how cars or other vehicles might be propelled by means of electricity. It extends from the main entrance at Brougham Street to the College entrance at the Meadow Walk, a distance of fully a quarter of a mile. It is laid with flat-footed girder rails, carried on cross sleepers, having a groove as in ordinary tramways, the pattern being Gowans's patent. The engine generating the necessary current is a 5-H.P. Portable Engine and Boiler by Messrs. Marshall & Sons, Gainsborough. The generating-machine, driven by engine, is a Series-wound dynamo, running about 700 revolutions per minute. The current of positive sign from this machine is led to a central rail of copper strips supported on wood, thereby insulating same from the earth. The negative pole of the dynamo is connected to the steel rails. The motor, which is carried on a four-wheeled coupled bogie, revolves at a speed of 1000 revolutions per minute, driving a countershaft by means of an endless belt, this countershaft being again geared to driving-wheels. The current is taken from the central rail or copper strip by means of a gun-metal wheel held in contact by a spiral spring. This wheel is connected to one pole of the motor, the other pole being connected through the driving-wheels to the steel rails, and thence back to the generator. It will be seen that the power is procured in a very simple and inexpensive way. The motor, which weighs only 7 cwt., has propelled two tram-cars, loaded with sixty-five passengers, at a speed of about nine miles an hour. It may be stated that since the railway was opened, it has worked without a hitch, and has carried upwards of 30,000 people, showing the interest taken by visitors in being carried along by electric power. The entire work of the electric railway has been designed and carried out by Messrs. King, Brown, & Co. of this city, and it ought to be specially noticed that the North Metropolitan Tramway Company of London very handsomely sent down two cars for use on the line.

For EU product safety concerns, contact us at Calle de José Abascal, 56–1°,
28003 Madrid, Spain or eugpsr@cambridge.org.

www.ingramcontent.com/pod-product-compliance
Ingram Content Group UK Ltd.
Pitfield, Milton Keynes, MK11 3LW, UK
UKHW012336130625
459647UK00009B/323